An ... to the Sincere Seeker

SRI SRI RAVI SHANKAR

VOLUME 1: JUNE 21, 1995—JUNE 13, 1996

ART OF LIVING FOUNDATION

An Intimate Note to the Sincere Seeker
SRI SRI RAVI SHANKAR

Art of Living Foundation
P.O. Box 50003
Santa Barbara, California 93150
Telephone: (805) 563-6396
Books and Tapes: (800) 574-3001; (503) 227-6411

Weekly Knowledge Coordinators: Bill Hayden, Anne Elixhauser

People from many countries sit with Sri Sri to participate and assist with the Weekly Knowledge. Next week it could be you.

Design, Type, and Production by David Burge, Gary Boucherle, and team: Brad Arnold, Denise Richardson, Ceci Balmer, Noelle Parnell Soares, Jerre Stetson, Mary Hunter Leach, and Laura Weinberg.

From a deep desire to share,
we present to you this
small treasure book
of wisdom from

Sri Sri Ravi Shankar

collected over the course of a year.
Every leaf in this album whispers
a new secret in the Art of Living.

Contents

Words are too small to convey the Truth
Yet they can trigger the flames of wisdom,
Shower comfort on the intense longing,
Raise cheers of joy and make you
Know I treasure your love for me.

Like God his creation,
The root its trunk,
Unknown, unheard, unseen,
In the silent chamber of heart
I am in you as you,
You are in me as me.

Ha! What a blessing!

—Sri Sri

A teacher may show you the Path, but rarely is there One who brings you back Home.

Here are the notes from Sri Sri Ravi Shankar that have helped guide many back Home, where gratitude is boundless.

We hope this collection will bring you Home, too.

This first volume contains the Weekly Knowledge from June 21, 1995 through June 13, 1996.

June 21, 1995 (Part I)
Big Sur, California

1 This Begins a New Practice

This begins a series of weekly notes of Knowledge from Sri Sri Ravi Shankar.

Beyond an event is Knowledge.
Beyond a person is Love.
Beyond an object is Infinity.

KNOWLEDGE IS NOT IN AN EVENT; IT IS BEYOND AN event. When you go beyond events, only then the truth dawns.

One particular event gives you a false notion. So you have to consider the totality of events, the totality of all events infinitely. Beyond the event is Knowledge.

A personality, a body, a mind, a complex of behaviors is changing. Love is unchanging. Beyond the person is love.

When you lose your personality, you become love. If you cannot lose yourself, you cannot find yourself! So, lose your personality; you'll find your Self!!!

Behind every object is infinity. An object is limited. Take an object and reduce, reduce, reduce, and you have an atom. An atom is infinity; each atom contains infinite space. Beyond the object is infinity.

The object behind the object is infinity. The person behind the person is love. *Maya* is getting caught up in the event, personality, or object. Knowledge, love, *Brahman** is seeing beyond the event, personality, or object. See? Just a little shift.

**Divine consciousness*

June 21, 1995 (Part II*)
Big Sur, California

2 Close to the Master

IF YOU'RE NOT FEELING CLOSE TO THE MASTER, IT'S BEcause of you. Because of your mind, because of your ego concepts. Share with the Master that which is very important or intimate to you. Share that. Do not feel shame, shy, or judgmental about yourself.

Unless you express to the Master that which is very intimate and important to you, just being on the formal and informal communication levels cannot make you feel close.

"How are you?" "Where are you going?" "How have you been?" Stop these formal and superficial conversations with the Master and speak with your heart that which is very important and intimate, very deep to your life. Don't just say how much the squash costs, 30 cents or whatever.

If you don't feel close to the Master, there's no point in having a Master. It is just another burden to you. You have enough already. Just say, "Goodbye."

Question: When you play little games and push us away, how can we feel close to you?

Sri Sri: You should feel *more* close if you are pushed away,

**Sri Sri thought to send out Weekly Knowledge notes, and everyone liked the idea —so this first week he sent two!*

scolded or ignored. Because to ignore somebody takes a lot of effort. When a Master does not even ignore wrapping paper or a flower that is in a vase, how can he ignore a walking, talking, breathing human being who is connected? How could that person be ignored? So when you understand this, you already feel close.

Torre: Can we call you every week?

*Kenny: Call Guruji*** *every week, and if he doesn't answer the phone, then you know you are loved!*

Sri Sri: Yes, put that in. *(laughter)*

You are with the Master to share the joy of the Master, to share the consciousness of the Master.

For this, you have to empty your cup of what is already in it.

Share whatever you have and don't judge, "Oh, that is garbage." The Master is ready to accept any garbage of any extent. However you are, he will embrace you.

He is ready to share. You only have to share from your side.

***People around the world commonly address Sri Sri as* Guruji *(honored teacher).*

June 29, 1995
California

3 Prabdha Karma and Sanchita Karma

SOME KARMA CAN BE CHANGED AND SOME CANNOT.

When you prepare a dessert, if sugar or ghee is less, you can add more. If some other ingredient is too much, it can all be adjusted and repaired. But once it is cooked, it cannot be reversed.

Milk can become sweet yogurt or sour yogurt, and sour yogurt can be sweetened. But neither can be reversed back to milk.

Sanchita karma can be changed and adjusted by spiritual practices. *Prabdha karma* cannot be changed. And *Satsang** burns the seed of all negative karmas before they are given a chance to sprout.

**When you praise someone,
you take on their good karma;**

**When you blame someone,
you take on their bad karma.**

**Know this and surrender both
good and bad karma to the Divine
and be free.**

**the company of the Master; also refers to any group of individuals who come together to celebrate in the Master's Knowledge*

July 4, 1995
Toronto, Ontario, Canada

4 Only Speak Knowledge

Only speak Knowledge. Don't repeat anything that someone tells you or opinions about anyone that someone states—that so-and-so said such-and-such about you. If someone comes to tell you such things, discourage them. Don't believe it.

If someone blames you directly, know that they are taking away your bad karma and let it go. Don't believe in it, and if you're one of the Master's close ones, you will take all the blame of the world with a smile.

Conflict is the nature of the world;
Comfort is the nature of the Self.
Amidst the conflict seek the comfort.

When you are bored with comfort, get into the games of the world. When you are tired of the games of the world, get into the comforts of the Self. If you are one of the Master's close ones, you do both simultaneously. Trying to end conflict prolongs it. Face the conflict by seeking the comfort of the Self.

God is alive in the world and has been putting up with all the ongoing conflicts throughout the ages. If God can put up with all the conflicts, you can too. The moment you agree to be with the conflict, the conflict disappears.

People who love peace do not want to fight, and those who fight do not love peace. Those who want peace want to run away. What is needed here is to be peaceful within and then fight. The whole message of the Gita is to be peaceful yourself and then fight. Krishna tells Arjuna to fight but be in peace at the same time. Does this ring a bell?

In the world, you resolve one conflict and another one comes up. For example, Russia is solved and then Bosnia arises. You make one better, and then another starts up. Your body gets a cold, then you get better; then your back hurts, then it gets better. Your body gets better, and then the mind goes. The world runs like this, isn't it?

Without any intention, misunderstandings happen. It's not up to you to try to resolve them. Ignore them and be alive!

July 12, 1995, *Guru Purnima** morning
Montreal Ashram, Canada

5 Master is a Doorway

MASTER IS A DOORWAY. AND THE DOORWAY NEEDS TO be more charming than the world so that you will come to the door. You are in the street and there is rain, thunder, hot sun; you need shelter. You look around, you find a doorway. You come to the door because it is more inviting, more charming, more celebrative, more joyful than anything else in the world.

You enter the door and see the world from there. This is a sign that you have come to the Master. Otherwise you may still be standing out in the street and looking at the door.

Once you have entered the door, then you will see the whole world from the eyes of the Master.

This means what? In every situation that you face, you will think *If this situation comes in front of the Master, how would he handle it? If this complication comes in front of the Master, how would he take it?*

The world looks much more beautiful—not a nasty place, but a place filled with love, filled with joy, cooperation, compassion, and all virtues. You will look at the world without any fear. You will relate to everybody without any fear.

From inside home, you will look at the thunder, you will look at the storm, you will look at the rain, you will look at the bright sun. Inside you have air conditioning. There is nothing that can really distract you, disturb you, or take the fullness

**the full moon day in July when one traditionally celebrates and honors the Master* away from you. Such a sense of security, such a sense of fullness and joy comes. That is the purpose of having a Master.

All relationships in the world go topsy-turvy. All relationships can get broken or made up and again broken. And there is craving and aversion. This is the world, this is *samsara.*

But the Master is not a relationship. The Master is the Presence. What is necessary is to feel the Presence of the Master. Don't make the Master a part of your world. "Oh, he looked at me." "He didn't look at me." "Oh, he said this." "He didn't say that." "Oh, somebody is close. I am not close." All this garbage comes into it.

Master is the Presence. World is relativity.

And relativity has limitations.

Presence is unlimited. Presence is vast, infinite, all-comprehensive, all-inclusive. And the Presence of the Master in your life will bring fulfillment to all your relations.

July 20, 1995
Montreal Ashram, Canada

6 Doubt

A DOUBT IS A GRAY AREA. GRAY IS SOMETHING WHICH IS neither white nor black. Now, how to solve the doubt?

Accept it either as black or as white.

Put it either as black and accept it, or as white and accept it —whether or not it is black or white. See the gray as black or white. Either way you accept it. Honest or dishonest—accept it. Then the mind is quiet. Then you are not in the gray area.

Put it in a category of white—no problem—doubt is not there. Put it in a category of black—no problem—accept. Have conviction: "I accept. They are dishonest and still part of me." That's it. Finished.

Doubt is wanting to get rid of something. Doubt is an ungrounded state with footing neither on this shore nor that shore. From there tension arises.

July 24, 1995
Montreal Ashram, Canada

7 Fire

THE SENSES ARE LIKE FIRE. YOUR LIFE IS ALSO LIKE FIRE. In the fire of senses, whatever you put in burns. If you burn tires, it creates pollution and bad smell. But if you burn sandalwood, it creates fragrance.

Celebration happens around the bonfire. Grief happens around the fire of cremation. The same fire that supports life in winter can also destroy. One fire, like a ghee lamp, lights your way and purifies. Another fire of toxic material creates pollution.

You are also like fire. Are you the fire that creates smoke and pollution—or the flame of camphor that creates light and fragrance?

A saint is like a camphor flame that creates light and the fragrance of love. He is the friend of life.

The fire that creates light and warmth and is useful is of higher quality. The fire that creates light and a little smoke is of medium quality. The fire that creates darkness and only smoke is of low quality. Learn to distinguish the different fires.

When your senses are engaged in goodness, then you will create light and fragrance; when engaged in impurity, you create smoke and darkness.

It is *sanyama* that transforms the quality of fire in you. Next week we will discuss sanyama.

July 30, 1995
Brookfield, Connecticut

8 Habits and Vows

HOW TO GET RID OF VASANAS (IMPRESSIONS)? THIS IS A question for all those who want to come out of habits.

You want to get rid of habits because they give pain and restrict you. The nature of vasana is to bother you or bind you, and wanting to be free is the nature of life.

Life wants to be free and when a soul doesn't know how to be free, it wanders through lifetimes wanting freedom.

The way to come out of habits is vows.

Take vows according to time and place. A vow should be time-bound. This brings good conduct and saves you from being wayward. Consider the time and place for vows to be taken.

For example, suppose someone has a habit of smoking cigarettes and says, "I will quit smoking," but cannot do it. They can take a vow—three months or 90 days—a time-bound vow. If someone is used to cursing and swearing, take a vow not to use bad language for ten days. Don't take it for a lifetime; you will break it immediately! If you happen to break it in between, don't worry. Just begin again. Slowly increase the duration until it becomes your nature.

This is *sanyama*. Everybody is endowed with a little sanyama.

When the mind dwells on useless thoughts, then two things happen:

One is that all those old patterns come up and you feel discouraged by them. You blame yourself and feel that you have not made any progress.

The second thing is that you see it as an opportunity for sanyama and feel happy about it. Without sanyama, life will not be happy and disease-free. For example, you know you should not eat three servings of ice cream or eat ice cream every day. If you do, you will get sick.

Habits will clog you when there is no liveliness or juice in your life. When you give a direction to your life force, you can rise above habits through sanyama.

All those habits which bother you, bind them in vows, in sanyama. So all those who are in Satsang, take a time-bound vow today and make a note of it. If you break a vow, make a note of it and share the time and date at the next Satsang. Continue it again. Tie those habits which bring you pain in sanyama.

August 10, 1995
Braunlage, Germany

9 Dealing with Blame

WHEN SOMEONE BLAMES YOU, WHAT DO YOU USUALLY DO? You blame them back or you put up resistance in yourself.

When someone blames you, they actually take away some negative karma from you. If you understand this you will feel happy about it.

When you put up resistance in your mind when someone blames you, you are not allowing them to take the negative karma, even if you don't react outwardly. You may resist *outside*, but *inside*—if you don't resist—you will feel immediately lighter. You feel happy: *Oh, good, somebody is there to blame me and take some negative karma.*

How does it feel to you when someone blames you? Do you feel some heaviness? Usually, when someone blames you, you feel hurt and you feel unhappy, you feel sad. This is all because you're...resisting. That is it. What you resist, persists.

You get hurt because you resist the blame.

When someone blames you, you resist it inside. Outside you may not resist, but inside when you resist, then that hurts you.

The ignorant person tells someone, "Don't blame me because it hurts me." An enlightened person also says, "Don't blame me." Do you know why? Because it might hurt *you*. They say this out of compassion. You can tell someone not to blame you out of compassion or out of anger.

✍ **News Flash:** *Sri Sri arrived in Poland for an enchanting course with nearly 400 people. Every eye filled with tears of gratitude. Then Guruji came to Braunlage, Germany, where more than 200 people are celebrating the silence.*

August 16, 1995
Rotterdam, Netherlands

10 Today is Krishna's Birthday: Birth of the Center of Attraction

KRISHNA MEANS *THE MOST ATTRACTIVE*. HE IS THE divinity that is the most attractive, the energy that pulls everything to it. Krishna is the formless center which is everywhere.

Any attraction from anywhere is coming only from Krishna.

Often people fail to see the spirit behind the attraction and merely hold on to the outer shell. And the moment you try to possess the shell, you will see Krishna has played a trick and you will be left with an empty shell in your hands and tears in your eyes.

Be clever like Radha—don't be tricked by Krishna. Krishna could not escape from Radha, for her whole world was filled with Krishna. If you can see that wherever there is an attraction, there is Krishna, then you are Radha; you are in your center.

The mind moves towards beauty, joy and truth. Krishna tells Arjuna, "I am the beauty in the beautiful, the strength in the strong, the wisdom in the wise." In this way he arrests the mind from moving away from him.

Krishna reveals this Knowledge to Arjuna because he is *anasuya*. Next week we will see what is anasuya.

August 24, 1995
London, United Kingdom

11 Anasuya

KNOWLEDGE WILL BE DIFFERENT AT DIFFERENT LEVELS OF consciousness. At a particular level of consciousness you will become *anasuya.*

Anasuya means being devoid of fault-finding eyes.

If a mirror is dusty, you need a duster to clean it. But if your eyes have a cataract, any amount of dusting will not help. So first you have to remove the cataract. Then you can see that the mirror is already clean.

There is a certain mind-set that always finds fault even in the best conditions in the world. When you give a person with this mind-set the best, they still find faults. Even with the best possible companion or the most beautiful painting, they will still find something wrong. That kind of mind-set cannot know the sacred Knowledge.

Krishna tells Arjuna that he is giving him the Royal Secret, because he is anasuya. "You are not finding fault in Me, even though you are so close." From a distance, even craters cannot be seen. Up close, even on a smooth surface there will be holes. If you are only interested in the holes, you will not see the magnanimity of things. If you are not in anasuya, Knowledge cannot blossom in you. Then there is no point in giving Knowledge.

Question: What about discrimination—wisdom?

If it is in your vision, you will find discrimination. Once you discover you have the wrong vision, half of the wrong vision has already disappeared.

There is a fine line here. There cannot be any better example than the cataract. Fault-finding is saying, "The whole world is not sharp, the whole world is no good." Anasuya is knowing, "It is my own vision of the world that is blurred."

The moment you are out of the Path, you find that everything was all wrong; that is not anasuya.

You have a friendship, and after ten years you decide to leave. When you leave, you do not see the good in that relationship. You find fault. This is not anasuya.

Suppose someone is coming in. It is windy, so you shut the door. But the person thinks the door has been slammed in his face! This is *asuya.* It is not anasuya.

Asuya is finding fault. It is seeing malicious intent everywhere. It is like a child who says, "Mother, you don't love me!" The child's vision is wrong. If the mother does not love the child, who will?

It is the same as if someone comes and says, "Guruji, you don't love me!" If I don't love them, forget about it. Nobody else in the world will! Where else will they find love? Nowhere.

A mother may get frustrated but not a Master.

August 31, 1995
Here and Now

12 The Love of the Ignorant, the Anger of the Enlightened

THE LOVE OF THE IGNORANT CAN BE HARMFUL, YET even the anger of the Enlightened is not harmful. It can be only good!

An example is the school at the Ashram in Bangalore. There are 250 children enrolled, but only 200 come to class on any given day. Fifty children don't show up. Why? Because they cry at home, "Mother, I don't want to go to school."

The mother says, "Oh, la la, don't cry...okay." She thinks *No child in the world is like my child.* And so she sticks up for the child and begins to speak for him. She does not see the teacher's point of view. So, what happens? The child grows up spoiled. The child will never learn the alphabet, never learn to read or write. But the mother says, "Oh, never mind, there are sheep to look after and fields to tend." The mother's love in ignorance has spoiled the child.

On the other hand,

The anger of the Enlightened is a blessing.

There are many instances of this in the Puranas. Once a Master was traveling in the middle province of India with a disciple following him a few yards behind. Some boys who were rude, rough, and abusive began to throw stones and tease the disciple, calling him names. This went on for some time as the boys followed the Master and the disciple.

They came to a river. The Master and the disciple got into a boat in order to cross. The boys got in another boat which started to sink in the middle of the river.

The Master slapped the disciple across the face. The disciple was so surprised, as he had not said a word back to the boys in response to their taunts. He had been such a good disciple and yet the Master had slapped him!

The Master said, "It is your fault. You are responsible for their boat sinking. You did not respond to their abuse. Nature has now punished them in a worse way because you did not have enough compassion to quell their insults."

The slap that the Master gave took away the karma of this event such that it would not be carried into the future of the boys. It also served to take away any little bit of joy the disciple may have felt at seeing the boys' boat sink! Thus, it also took away the karma of the event for the disciple.

So, the anger of the Enlightened is a blessing!

September 6, 1995
Bangalore Ashram, India

13 A Liar is Innocent

A DEAR PERSON WHOM YOU TRUST LIES TO YOU AND GETS caught. What do you feel?

1. Sadness
2. Anger
3. Cheated
4. Disappointment
5. Compassion
6. Let down
7. Loss of respect
8. Wonder
9. Shock
10. Embarrassment

Recently when someone lied to me, I felt happy and more love, for they were not a good liar. Had they been a good liar, they would not have been caught. I thought *They were so innocent that they could not even lie properly.* They lied and got caught! If they had not been caught, how would you know they were a liar?

So...you can never know a good liar.

The person you call a liar is not a good liar and they are innocent. Aren't they?

And so...*(laugh)*, you need not go through all the listed mental gymnastics. Instead melt and dissolve in Love.

September 13, 1995
Melbourne, Australia

14 Be a Gopal

Like fish in the water, you are in air. Thoughts are in mind. Mind is in Big Mind. The Big Mind in Me is love. Emotions are ripples in love. Love is all Knowledge.

Every atom of Big Mind is crammed with Knowledge. Knowing this, you stop seeking.

You seek until you come to the Master.

You walk until you come to the swimming pool. You don't walk or run in the swimming pool—you swim or float. Once you come to the Master, seeking stops, blossoming begins.

You are Knowledge. Every atom in you is shimmering with Knowledge. This is called *go. Go* has four meanings:

- Knowledge
- Movement
- Achievement
- Freedom or liberation

Pal means *friend* or *protector*—one who takes care of. Be a *Go-pal;* be a friend in Knowledge.

Often you become friends by:

- Gossiping about negative things
- Complaining
- Similar cravings or aversions

- Common enemies or common problems
- Common goals or common addictions

You become friends because you have something in common. Coming together in Knowledge is rare. Be a friend in Knowledge. Uplift each other in Knowledge.

All Satsangees are Gopals—reminding each other, coming together in Knowledge for Knowledge. That is Gopal.

Be a protector of this Knowledge.

September 21, 1995
Bangalore Ashram, India

15 Silence

Prayer within breath
Is silence
Love within Infinity
Is silence
Wisdom without word
Is silence
Compassion without aim
Is silence
Action without doer
Is silence
Smiling with all the Existence
Is silence!

September 27, 1995
Bangalore Ashram, India

16 Big Mind

You know there is a big and a small mind. Sometimes the Big Mind wins over the small mind and sometimes it is the other way around.

When the small mind wins over, it is misery, and when the Big Mind wins, it is joy. Small mind promises joy and leaves your hand empty. Big Mind may bring resistance in the beginning but fills you with joy.

The word *Guru* means *great.*

Jaya means *victory.*

Deva means *the Divine who is fun-loving, playful, light.* One who is playful is often not dignified and when one is dignified, he is often not playful.

Jai Guru Dev means victory to the Greatness in you, victory to the Big Mind in you that is both dignified and playful.

You need not say victory or hail to the Master, as he has won over already!! You say victory to your own Self, your own Mind, over the wailing small mind.

October 5, 1995
Bangalore Ashram, India

17 The Only Thing You Must Remember

THE ONLY THING YOU MUST REMEMBER IS HOW FORTUNATE you are. When you forget this, you become sad.

Sorrow indicates:
1) your negative qualities, and
2) your attachment to your positive qualities.

When you think you are too good, you blame the world; then you become sad. The purpose of sorrow is to bring you back to the Self. And Self is all Joy. But this is possible only through Knowledge—awareness.

Knowledge or awareness leads sorrow towards the Self. With lack of Knowledge, the same sorrow multiplies and does not get completed. Knowledge completes sorrow.

With the power of Knowledge you transcend sorrow.

In this Path you have everything. We have this beautiful Knowledge which has all the flavors in it—wisdom, laughter, service, silence, singing, dancing, humor, celebration, yagyas, caring, complaints(!), problems(!), complications(!), and chaos to add color.

Life is so colorful!

October 10, 1995
Bangalore Ashram, India

18 Freedom and Discipline

FREEDOM AND DISCIPLINE ARE OPPOSITES AND COMPLEMENTARY.

The purpose of defense is to protect freedom, but is there freedom in defense? Do soldiers have freedom? No, they are totally bound, not even allowed to put the right foot down when told the left foot. Their steps are measured and they are unable even to walk with a natural rhythm. There is total lack of freedom in defense. That which has absolutely no freedom is protecting the freedom of the country!

Discipline protects freedom. They both go hand in hand. Understand this and go ahead in life. You have some restrictions and it is this that allows you freedom. You can choose to focus either on freedom or discipline, and this makes you happy or unhappy. Freedom without discipline is like a country without a defense.

Fences should be fences; a fence cannot be built all over the property. If your fence is all over, how can you build on the property? That state of high, absolute freedom is too difficult;

we need to be very practical. Yes, there is a state of unlimited bliss, the freedom *Advaita** talks about. The Advaita Knowledge has been totally misused or used according to one's own fancies and conveniences. There must be awareness in the mind, love in the heart, and righteousness in action.

Love and fear are two possibilities that put you on track. The Jewish religion put fear as the main thing so that life could improve.

Nature induces fear at a certain age in a child. When a child is very young, it gets 100% time and love of the mother. The child has no fear. As the child grows more independent, it becomes cautious. Nature brings in an iota of fear. With freedom, the child starts walking carefully.

Fear of losing freedom brings defense. The purpose of defense is to eliminate fear.

On this Path, Knowledge is your freedom—and also your defense.

**the non-dual philosophy of the Upanishads expounded in detail by* Adi Shankara

October 17, 1995
Halifax, Nova Scotia, Canada

19 Discipleship Ends

KNOWLEDGE HAS AN END. KNOWLEDGE COMPLETES.

So also does discipleship, for the disciple is aimed at acquiring Knowledge.

Once you cross the water, however nice the boat is, you get off the boat. After twelve years, the disciple completes his studies. The master does a ceremony called *Samavartha,* when he tells the disciple that he is ending the discipleship and asking him to behave at par with him and let the Brahman dynamically manifest.

Sakha is a companion in life and death; it never ends. In the path of love there is neither beginning nor end. Sakha only wants the beloved. He doesn't care about the Knowledge or liberation. Love is incomplete because of longing! And so it is infinite, for infinity can never be complete.

Arjuna was a sakha to Krishna and although Krishna was the perfect Master, he was a sakha, too.

What are you:
a shishya (disciple),
or a sakha (companion)?

October 24, 1995
Montreal Ashram, Canada

20 Sakha: Your Reliable Sense

There are three things: the Self, the senses, and the object (the world). And there are three words: *sukha,* pleasure; *duhkha,* sorrow; and *sakha,* companion. These have one thing in common: *kha,* which means *senses.*

The Self through the senses experiences the world. When the senses are with the Self, that is pleasure (sukha), because the Self is the source of all joy or pleasure. When the senses are away from the Self (duhkha)—in the mud, lost in the object—that is misery. Mud, misery, mind—they are very close.

World		Self
Sorrow	← Senses ("Kha") →	Joy
(Duhkha)		(Sukha)

Self is the nature of joy. In any pleasant experience, you close your eyes: you smell a nice flower, or you taste or touch something. Sukha is that which takes you to the Self.

Duhkha is that which takes you away from the Self. Sorrow simply means that you are caught up in the object, which goes on changing, instead of focusing on the Self.

All the sense objects are just a diving board to take you back to the Self.

Sa-kha, companion, means *He is the senses.* Sakha is one who has become your senses, who is your senses. It means I get Knowledge through you; you are my sixth sense. As I trust my mind, so I trust you. A friend could be just an object of the senses, but a sakha has become the very senses.

Sakha is the companion who is there in the experiences of both duhkha and sukha. It means *one who leads you back to the Self.* If you are stuck in an object, that wisdom which pulls you back to the Self is sakha. Knowledge is your companion and your companion is Knowledge.

The Master is the embodiment of Knowledge. Sakha means, "He is my senses, I see the world through that Wisdom, through Him."

If your sense is the Divine, then you see the whole world through the Divinity.

Your head will be in the mud in a few years; don't put mud in your head while you are still alive!!

✍ **News Flash:**

Sri Sri spoke at the United Nations 50th Anniversary Celebration on October 22. Here are a few quotes:

Spiritual education is needed to uncover the knowledge that we are, first, part of the Divine, and second, we are human beings.

In this age, even when technology has advanced so far, we have cared very little for the emotional and spiritual needs of people. Neither at home nor in school have we been taught how to release negative emotions. Either we worry about the past or the future, or we get stuck in negativity.

A stress-free mind and disease-free body are the birthrights of every human being. Only true spiritual knowledge can help us to handle our mind and bring us back to the present moment.

Breathing techniques, meditation, and yoga can be used as powerful tools to release tensions and negative emotions, enabling one to live more fully in the present moment.

November 1, 1995
London, United Kingdom

21 Skepticism

IGNORANCE IS BEING A SKEPTIC AND NOT KNOWING YOU are a skeptic. If you think you are a skeptic, you are no longer a skeptic! You have a clue of something beyond. So, in reality, you can never know whether you are a skeptic or not!

A skeptic is stuck in a paradigm and closes all other possibilities. But this creation contains all possibilities. As one understands the paradigm shift, skepticism is removed.

A real scientist can never afford to be a skeptic because skepticism closes down possibilities and does not continue to probe into unknown areas of existence.

In short, skepticism is an "I know it all" attitude, and this attitude is unscientific. Skepticism is dispelled by Knowledge.

In every human being, deep inside there is faith and love. What you think is skepticism is only a thin layer. If you hold in your mind *They are skeptics*, you empower their skepticism.

Do not recognize someone's skepticism and try to argue with them. Argument strengthens their skepticism. Fear of interference in one's freedom brings more resistance and causes more skepticism.

Your silence and the smile from your heart will dispel their skepticism. There is nothing better than silence to break skepticism. Silence means the quality of consciousness, not just keeping lips tight.

Skepticism comes only in people who walk with boundaries. Children have no skepticism. They live in their fantasy world, a world of many possibilities. Their world is one of innocence, joy, beauty, and so much love.

November 9, 1995
New Delhi, India

22 Shaucha and Ashaucha

When you are miserable, what has happened? You have gone away from the Self. This is called *ashaucha*. It means you have become unclean.

In India when someone dies, the close relatives are said to be ashaucha for ten days because they are very sad. They are impure because they have moved away from the Self. After ten days of just being with that experience and reading the Gita, being with the Knowledge, and pulling themselves back into the Self, then it is called *shaucha*. They have purged out the impurities that have come during those events.

This keeps happening again and again in dealings in life. You become ashaucha and you have to get back to shaucha. Go deeper in to yourself, then real shaucha happens.

Shaucha's benefits are clarity in the intellect, a pleasing mind, focused awareness in the mind, a say over the senses, and therefore eligibility to realize the Self.

Shaucha is being disinterested in the tendencies of one's own senses. If a tendency in your body arises, just have the understanding *Oh yes, here is this old familiar tendency coming up again. Come on, you have had this experience enough, and still the body is craving for it again.* Being disinterested in one's own body—just an idea, a sort of distaste—and in one moment the situation changes.

Why do people love each other so much, have such an intimate relationship, and then fight? Ashaucha has happened. *If you don't get distaste for the tendency of the senses, then distaste for the object of the senses will come; you will blame the object.*

When ashaucha happens, then come back to shaucha quickly. Suppose you get drowned in any worldly aspect, just know this is ashaucha... *That is why I am suffering misery.* Then come back to shaucha.

Your attraction or craving is only as long as you think someone is "other." When you think they are part of you or your Self, then the attraction dies out. That is why a husband or wife is not attracted to the partner but to someone else—because the partner has already become a part of them.

When you realize everyone is part of your Self, you enjoy the whole world without a sense of craving.

November 15, 1995
Bangalore Ashram, India

23 Boredom and Sadhana

WHAT IS BOREDOM?

A repetition without interest or love causes a monotonous state of mind; that is boredom. It overshadows the Self.

Spiritual practices *(sadhana)* are again a repetition whose purpose is to destroy the boredom and reunite with the Self. A practice itself creates boredom; as you continue, it penetrates the boredom and destroys it once and for all. Whether the practice gives you joy or boredom, it must be continued. Only your practices, your sadhana, can overcome the mind.

Self is Love and Love is always repetitive. That is why love letters are simply repetitive and yet there is no boredom there. If you are bored with yourself, then how much more boring are you for others?

Root out the boredom in you through deep and continued meditation. Wake up and walk up.

November 23, 1995
Bangalore Ashram, India

24 Who Are You: Brahma, Vishnu, Shiva, or Guru?

There are three forces: Brahma shakti, Vishnu shakti, and Shiva shakti. You may have one of these predominant. Brahma shakti is the force to create something new. Vishnu shakti is maintenance. Shiva shakti is bringing in transformation, infusing new life, or destroying.

Some of you have Brahma shakti. You may create well, but you may not be able to maintain. For example, you may make friends very fast, but it does not last long.

There are others who cannot create but are good at maintaining. For example, people have long-lasting friendships but cannot make any new friends. In such cases, Vishnu shakti is dominant.

And then there are others who have more of Shiva shakti. They bring in new life or transformation—or they can destroy the whole set up.

With Guru shakti, all three shaktis have blossomed fully.

So each of you first identify which shakti you have more of and aspire for Guru shakti.

Guru makes a group,
but a group cannot make a Guru.

November 29, 1995
Bangalore Ashram, India

25 How to Maintain Intimacy

INTIMACY OFTEN GETS BROKEN BECAUSE OF EGO OR YOUR desire. What breaks intimacy?

- Ego or taking a position
- Desire
- Taking intimacy for granted
- Finding imperfection in oneself or others
- Expectations
- Insensitivity or over-sensitivity
- Lack of *vivek* or *vairagya* (discretion or dispassion)
- Judgments
- Grumbling or lack of gratitude

Dissolving into infinity is the way to maintain intimacy. Intimacy is dissolving into infinity. Dissolving into infinity brings you to the moment. Go beyond events.

Dissolve into infinity, be in the moment, and look beyond the events.

This is the way to maintain intimacy.

✍ *If you attend Satsang, you don't get much; but if you don't, you lose a lot. Just to maintain where you are, what you are, you need to attend weekly Satsang.*

Now, start doing ten minutes of Satsang each day, sharing the Knowledge with someone—anyone. You are so used to talking gossip. Now for two weeks, talk Knowledge, especially to those not coming to Satsang.

This is an exercise: Every day for ten minutes, do individual Satsang and skillfully talk ten minutes of Knowledge.

Say, "Everything is temporary, everything is changing." Speak some Knowledge on the changing nature of the world.

December 7, 1995
Bangalore Ashram, India

26 All are searching for sweets; the One who finds them gives them away

SRI SRI WAS ON THE PORCH WITH A GROUP OF PEOPLE. He sent Kashi to get the sweets from inside the *kutir,** but Kashi returned saying he could not find them. He went again and again, three times, and still he could not find them. Then Guruji himself went in. He came out with the sweets and gave them to everyone.

This is exactly what happens in life. Many want sweetness in life. Some are searching hard, but only one finds. And when that one finds, he gives to everyone.

Everyone is blissed in, and some are blissed out, too!

**a cottage or bungalow*

December 14, 1995
Bangalore Ashram, India

27 Overcoming Events

ALL THE PROBLEMS THAT YOU FACE IN LIFE ARE BEcause you attach over-importance to the events. The events grow bigger while you remain smaller.

Say, for example, you are riding a motorbike on a busy motorway and in front of you there is another vehicle emitting exhaust fumes. You have three options:

1. You can complain, somehow bear with it, and still follow the vehicle.
2. You can slow down or wait for some time to allow the vehicle to move far away from you.
3. You can use your skill, overtake the vehicle, and forget about it.

As in the first case, most of you stick on the events and are miserable, like inhaling fumes throughout your journey.

In the second case, you don't get permanent relief, as another bigger vehicle might come in front of you. Running away from events is not the permanent solution.

Wise people use their skill to surmount the event. If the vehicle is in perfect condition the skill is effective. Conditioning the vehicle is sadhana—practice. And skill is the grace of the Guru.

The mistakes you have made in the past have made you humble; you need not make mistakes in the future to become humble.

December 21, 1995
Gyanmandir, Bangalore, India

28 The Washing Machine

OUR BODY IS LIKE A WASHING MACHINE. OUR MIND IS LIKE cloth. Love is like pure water. Knowledge is detergent. Each lifetime is one wash cycle.

The mind comes into the body to get cleansed and pure. But if you put in mud instead of detergent, your clothes become dirtier than before. You will have to go on putting clothes in the washing machine to get them cleaned. And the process repeats again and again. Similarly, you will have many more births until you stop repeating the mistakes that you have made.

December 27, 1995
Weggis, Switzerland

29 Divine is All Celebration

A POOR MAN CELEBRATES THE NEW YEAR ONCE A YEAR. A rich man celebrates each day. But the richest man celebrates every moment.

How rich are you? Do you celebrate once a year? Once a month? Every day? If you celebrate every moment, you are the Lord of Creation.

Review the year while you celebrate. This is your homework. What did you do? What did you achieve? How useful were you this past year?

Sit for an hour and think about every week, one minute per week, and see the year's growth in less than an hour. With a flower, on New Year's Day, offer the whole year to the Divine.

Spreading the Fragrance

During Satsang, Sri Sri opened a small, nicely-wrapped present —a tiny bottle of jasmine perfume. He twisted off the cap and sniffed the lovely fragrance. He proceeded to pour a small amount on some paper, which he waved in the air, wafting the scent to all corners of the hall. Everyone could then enjoy it.

Guruji explained that it is not enough simply to have the fragrance. We have to know how to spread it. Flowers have fragrance, but it is the wind that spreads it. In the same way, each one of us is wonderful within—we are beautiful, caring, and loving. But we need to know how to spread the fragrance.

Satsang is that wind that spreads this fragrance to everyone.

January 5, 1996
Weggis, Switzerland

30 New Year's Celebration

New Year's was a grand celebration...like every day! And everyone was unusually crazy...like every day! Sri Sri was fantastically charming...like every day!

And a basket full of chocolates was on the couch...like every day! They were in the shape of bees today. And they started flying from the Guru's hand.

JUST BE

Joy is dissolving...losing your identity.
Rest is dissolving...losing your identity.
Love is dissolving...losing your identity.
The message for 1996 is...JUST BE!
Relax and just be.

That doesn't mean be lazy...no!
Be very busy...and just be.

The events come and go, they perish like flowers.
But every event and every person contains
some honey.
Like a bee, just take the honey out of every
event and every moment—and move on.
Be like a busy bee and be in the Being.

Question: What is the nectar of life?
Sri Sri: The Infinity...the Divinity.

January 11, 1996
Weggis, Switzerland

31 Wrapping Paper

ALL SENSORY PLEASURES IN THE WORLD ARE LIKE WRAPping paper; the true bliss is the Presence inside.

Divine love is the present, yet we are holding onto the paper believing we have already enjoyed the gift. It's like putting the chocolate inside your mouth with the paper still on. A little chocolate may seep into the mouth, but the covering makes sores in the mouth.

Unwrap the present. The whole world is there for you to enjoy. The wise know how to enjoy the gift inside, while the ignorant get stuck with the paper.

✍ *Wally told Guruji: I have some property for you to consider as an Ashram in the U.S.*

Sri Sri: I want every home to be an Ashram.

How many of you consider your home to be an Ashram? If not, what keeps your home from being an Ashram? What are the impediments? What do you think are the qualities of an Ashram?

January 16, 1996
Ljubljana, Slovenia

32 Is Guru Satisfied or Unsatisfied?

A STUDENT'S JOB IS TO SATISFY THE MASTER. But how can you satisfy someone who is already satisfied?

If Guru is satisfied, then your growth is shunned.

If Guru is unsatisfied, he's away from the Self.

If Guru is satisfied, then what can inspire you to grow?

If he's unsatisfied, he cannot be a Guru.

If he's satisfied, he cannot be a Guru.

So what is the answer?

✍ **News Flash:**

The Master arrived for the first time on January 15 in the Croatian capital of Zagreb. As soon as we landed, we drove him straight to one of the largest concert halls in Zagreb. Sri Sri first met with a group of over a hundred professionals, including doctors and members of the press. A few hours later, the hall filled to capacity for his evening lecture. The national television station filmed the talk. Before addressing the large crowd, Sri Sri went out to the lobby to greet over a hundred people who were unable to enter. His exquisite talk saturated the atmosphere with a soft feeling of grace and peace. At the end of the lecture, many still waited outside for over two hours to get a glimpse of Sri Sri.

The next evening Guruji gave his very first talk in Ljubljana, Slovenia. Hundreds crowded into the World Trade Center and soon overloaded Guruji with flowers. He continued to talk for an hour and a half as the enthusiastic crowd would not let him finish. Immense gratitude and celebration charged the atmosphere. The Art of Living groups in Croatia and Slovenia did an excellent job.

Sri Sri now flies off to New York for a television interview and then it's on to the Advanced Course in Hawaii!

January 24, 1996
Kaua'i, Hawaii

33 Advice from Hawaii

WHAT TYPE OF TIME DO YOU GIVE THE DIVINE? USUALLY you give the time that is leftover, when you have nothing else to do, when no guests are coming, there are no parties to go to, no nice movies to watch, no weddings to attend. Such time you give. This is not quality time.

Give quality time to the Divine. It will be rewarded. If your prayers are not answered it is because you have never given quality time. *Give Satsang and meditation your highest priority.*

Give prime time to the Divine.

You definitely will be rewarded.

✍ **News Splash:**

Here in Hawaii we're enjoying a fun-filled course this week, for you know **God Loves Fun**. *The first copies arrived of the long-awaited book,* **Sri Sri Ravi Shankar: The Way of Grace**, *and David and Gary presented them to Guruji.*

Satsang is open to the public each evening. The huge waves of the Hawaiian shores cannot compete with the waves of bliss at Satsang. Sri Sri brought out deep Knowledge from the most mundane questions. We will bring out these tapes for you soon.

✍ **Riddle:** *What is most freely given yet not taken?*

1. *Compliments?...no.*
2. *Blame?...no, people take blame.*
3. *Money?...no, money is readily taken, not freely given.*
4. *Happiness?...nobody can give happiness.*
5. *??*

Clue: It hangs in space like an orphan. No one owns it. Like an overripe papaya in Hawaii, it rots. The answer to this riddle lies in the beginning. ALOHA!

February 1, 1996
Honolulu, Hawaii

34 The Most Beautiful Spot in the Universe

THERE IS A PLACE YOU CAN COME WHERE EVERYTHING is beautiful. Tourists go from place to place looking for beauty. They try to take beauty from that place. They only get tired and tanned. Yet the most beautiful spot anywhere is right here. When you come here, you find that wherever you are, everything is so beautiful.

Where is this place?
Don't look here and there; come within you.
When you are here, then any place becomes beautiful.
Then wherever you go, you add beauty there.

If you are unhappy, even the moon is irritating to you, sweet things are nauseating, music is disturbing. When you are calm and centered inside, noise is musical, clouds are magical, rain is liquid sunshine.

Book yourself on a trip to this most beautiful place in the universe. Then you'll find that every day is a vacation and a celebration.

✍ **News Splash from the surf:**

A lady driving along the coast of Kaua'i just started singing our bhajans which she had never heard before. Later, she found herself at our Satsang.

A Hawaiian Princess, Owana, wondered why she felt compelled to drive in circles around a hotel in Honolulu. She later discovered from a devotee that it was Sri Sri's hotel. The next night she was singing her deeply felt native Hawaiian songs at Sri Sri's feet.

On Sunday, a woman named Mary spent the day at an ancient temple site (heiau). She had gone there to pray; her prayer was to meet her spiritual teacher and be shown the way Home. The next day she met Sri Sri and instantly became devoted.

P.S. The answer to last week's riddle is "advice." Advice hangs in space, the giver goes on giving, the taker never takes. It goes on and on...

February 8, 1996
Miami Beach, Florida

35 Indebtedness or Abundance?

QUESTION: GOD IS ALL-ABUNDANT, ALL-FULL, AND WE ARE all connected to God. Then why are we in debt, except for some? Why do they have, and we don't have?

Sri Sri: Is it only money? You have abundance, yet at the same time, you are indebted. So how can both be true?

Someone in the group: An abundance of indebtedness!

Sri Sri: When you say you are indebted, that means you have received. Otherwise how can you be indebted? So be thankful for being indebted. Those who have received should feel indebted.

Feel indebted. Feel gratitude.
Then abundance comes.

Abundance and indebtedness coexist. You think you are indebted, but you really are not. Yet it is better to feel totally indebted, because every bit of what you have doesn't belong to you, including your body. When you are infinitely indebted for your body, for Knowledge, for things you have received, and for your own life, then you bask in the abundance of the Creator.

Someone in the group: I feel very indebted. Thank you!

News Flash:

Physicians of Apple Valley, California, organized memorable meetings and Satsangs. Sri Sri appeared on CNN News and in the local media and newspapers for several days before the much-awaited event. Local TV made announcements every hour.

From there to electrifying Satsangs in packed halls in Los Angeles. Divya and the drummers got everyone on their feet.

A funny thing happened at the Los Angeles airport. When Sri Sri went through the metal detector, the alarm went off. He took off his shawl which contained a gold brocade and again tried to pass through. Again the alarm went off! Of course, he wasn't wearing a belt or any such thing. Someone suggested that it could be his mala (beads). With an amused smile, he removed it, yet off went the alarm again! Now there was not much left for Guruji to take off. The guard was perplexed. Politely, he asked Guruji to step aside for a metal check with a hand-held device. After a couple of tries, they found him "clean" and let him pass. With everyone applauding, Guruji came out giggling.

Lloyd and his students organized 700 people to welcome the Master at the University of Northeast Missouri.

In Fort Lauderdale, the church filled with decorations and devotion, Knowledge and grace. The hurricane of sattva has moved on to Miami.*

**purity, righteousness*

February 14, 1996
London, United Kingdom

36 Abiding in the Self

ABIDING IN THE SELF YOU BECOME THE VALENTINE for the whole world. Spirit is the valentine of matter and matter is the valentine of the spirit. They are made for each other. They uphold each other. If you hold onto matter and do not respect the spirit, then matter is not pleased. If you honor the spirit, then you will care for the world, and when you care for the world, it will take care of you.

I am the valentine of the whole world and I reside in every heart. If you are my valentine, you will see me everywhere.

Have the same love for everyone, with different flavors. You cannot behave the same way with everyone, but you can love all of them the same. Love transcends behavior and etiquette.

✍ **News Flash:**

Just a week before Sri Sri's arrival, Raj woke up in the middle of the night in Loughborough. He thought that some light was coming from the clock. He looked at Sri Sri's picture and saw light coming from it. This light grew and filled the room. He made sure that there was no outside light left on. The divine light stayed on for about ten minutes.

Upholland, Lancashire held an Advanced Course in Sri Sri's presence.

Sri Sri gave a talk on "Ayurveda and the Art of Living" at the Liverpool Medical Institution. The hall was packed—standing room only. Guruji gave a brilliant talk, but he thought it was mundane!

Sri Sri's entourage moved with luggage and cars at its own speed and proceeded to Stourbridge in the Midlands for an event organized by Stourbridge Earth Mysteries. Guruji's talk was simply great! We moved on to London, arriving at 3 o'clock in the morning for "The UK Tired of Living Teachers Meeting" with baggage, blankets, pillows, plastic bags, pots and pans, and the usual divine chaos!!

February 21, 1996
Oslo, Norway

37 Knowledge and Faith

In science you have knowledge first, then faith follows. In spirituality, faith comes first, then Knowledge follows.

For example, the knowledge that pesticides and chemical fertilizers are good for plants came through science, and people had faith in it, and all over the world they were used. And then another knowledge came that they were not good and the faith shifted to organic farming. The same with antibiotics.

The knowledge brought faith, the knowledge changed, and then faith changed. The knowledge and faith of science is from a "happening."

In spirituality, faith is first and Knowledge comes later. Like *Sudarshan Kriya, pranayama, yoga asanas,* and *meditation**—first you have faith and then Knowledge follows. For example, if you do pranayama faithfully, then you get the Knowledge of the prana; if you do your meditation faithfully, the Knowledge of consciousness follows. Even an illiterate, through faith, attains deep Knowledge.

Science considers even human beings as matter; spirituality considers even earth as mother, even rivers and mountains as living beings.

****Sudarshan Kriya:*** *see page 94;* ***pranayama:*** *breathing techniques that energize and invigorate mind and body, learned on Healing Breath Workshop (see page 94);* ***yoga asanas:*** *natural postures that improve health and well-being;* ***meditation:*** *see page 95.*

Science regards life as matter,
Spirituality regards even matter as life.

✍ **News Flash:**

Sri Sri celebrated Shivaratri at the German Academy. Devotees put their hearts and souls into making the place so beautiful. The puja and Satsang transported everyone to another plane. As usual, laughter filled the corridors of the new Ashram. The big hall is already too small, to the surprise of everyone! Our own spring water replaced Pepsi and Coke!

The night before we left, Lakshmi called Sri Sri from Norway. Guruji said we would arrive at the airport at exactly 12:15. It kept Lakshmi wondering and confused because she expected us almost an hour earlier than that.

The next day, the giggling gang made their way to the airport but had left some luggage behind at the hotel. The flight was conveniently delayed—very unusual for SAS airlines. We retrieved the missing luggage and we all arrived in Norway— at 12:15 on the dot!

February 29, 1996
Bangalore Ashram, India

38 Respect

WHY DO YOU RESPECT SOMEONE? BECAUSE OF THEIR good qualities, isn't it? For example, positive qualities like honesty, wisdom, love, talents, behavior. But all these change in time. And when they do change, you lose respect. You only respect the greatness.

I have tremendous respect for each and every one. Not for their greatness or wisdom or talent, but for their very person. I respect everyone totally. So I can never lose respect for anybody, however they may be.

One doesn't need to be great in order to be respected. Respecting the life makes you great.

Don't look for respect from others; that makes you weak.

Have respect for the Self and no one can take your self-respect.

News Flashes:

From Norway:

Plastered with big posters of Sri Sri, Ingrid's van caught the attention of traffic. Posters were all over Oslo; Sheila made a poster crusade.

Vinod and Ingrid turned a reluctant ambassador into an enthusiastic devotee who stayed up all night reading the book **Sri Sri Ravi Shankar: The Way of Grace**.

Adventure time: We all went to a ski simulator and then sledded three kilometers downhill. Everyone tumbled down into the snow, our hands and feet frozen. It was -10°C, everyone was wearing heavy winter clothes, but there was Guruji, sledding with sandals and shawl. He didn't get a speck of snow on himself.

Then on to Copenhagen—the capital of Denmark:

It was a media event: people from TV, radio, and the newspaper queued into the hotel and the TV crew followed us to packed and lively public talks.

From Stockholm, Sweden:

A TV crew came to the meditation hall to interview Sri Sri. They asked what he thought about the New Age and if Art of Living was part of the New Age. With a vivid smile, Sri Sri replied, "Age is always new."

One of Sweden's most respected TV journalists for a major TV channel featured Sri Sri and the Dalai Lama.

Evening talks bubbled with humor, brilliant questions, and laughter. All the "hard nuts" started popping like popcorn. As usual, the best talks are never recorded.

The Master arrived on February 28 in Bangalore without his baggage. And he said that is how he came to the world—without any baggage!

March 6, 1996
Bangalore Ashram, India

39 Desire and Joy

ALL DESIRES ARE FOR HAPPINESS. THAT IS THE GOAL OF desire, isn't it? How often does your desire lead you to the goal?

But have you thought about the nature of desire? It simply means tomorrow and not now, isn't it?

Joy is never tomorrow. It is always now.

How can you have desires when you are joyful? And how can you really be joyful now when you have desires?

Desire appears to lead you to happiness. In fact it cannot. And that is why it is *maya*.*

What do you say?

News Flash:

Participants from all corners of India attended an Advanced Course from March 1-5. The Ashram bustled with activity. Despite a large number of young devotees, the course was unusually silent. The silence broke with the boisterous celebration of Holi, the Festival of Colors.

We held Satsang in the open air with the sound of drums, the beat of our hearts, the radiant full moon soaking us in bright colors, and our laughter and tears.

*illusion

March 13, 1996
Swargashram (Heavenly Abode), Rishikesh, India

40 Faith and Love

GOD DOES NOT WISH YOU TO HAVE MORE FAITH BECAUSE the more faith you have, the more work for God. God will have to run behind you; then you start controlling Him. He is the servant of faithful servants and He does not want too many servants telling Him what He should be doing!

Love is the highest strength, yet it makes you absolutely weak. So God—Enlightened One—Nature—does not want you to have more faith or love. With too much faith and love, you make God weak.

So, it is better for God that you have less faith. Things go on as they are. Why transform? Be happy.

Meditation is seeing God in yourself.
Love is seeing God in the person next to you.
Knowledge is seeing God everywhere.

Expression of love is service.
Expression of joy is your smile.
Expression of peace is meditation.
Expressing God is conscious action.

News Flash:

Everything was meticulously planned and organized before Sri Sri arrived in Delhi. At the airport, a spontaneous Satsang developed as airport personnel and other passengers also joined in. Then the well-organized plans went haywire and the usual divine chaos followed. Everything was settled in a flash but the organizers were left holding their plans on paper!

At Saritha Vihar Satsang, the sweets and flowers made a carpet in the large hall that matched the fragrance of joy and celebration.

The next day at Karol Bagh, the authorities had more than one reason to raise their eyebrows—traffic jams on the roads, a stampede in the hall, and people forgetting their families in their eagerness to follow the "Gurumobile." Then on to Rishikesh and the Teachers Refresher Course.

Rishikesh: the lush green Himalayas; the holy Ganges roars, gurgles, sometimes murmurs; peacocks call in the early morning; temple bells chime at sunrise; the chant of Vedic hymns at all times; dips in the cold waters, everyone shedding shawls and sweaters on their way in, leaving most reluctantly; sitting with the Master in the evening, watching the sunset; electrifying Satsangs; discourses on the Bhagavad Gita in Hindi by Sri Sri; a time that transported everyone...

March 20, 1996
Swargashram (Heavenly Abode), Rishikesh, India

41 Questions & Dealing with Desire

A boy asked a question, and before Sri Sri could answer, he was ready with another question.

To this Guruji said,

"If you hold on to the question, how will you receive the answer?"

Give away the question to me and then you will find that you are in the answer.

Desires arise on their own…don't they? They ask you before they come. When they come, what do you do with them? If you say that you don't want to have any desires, then it becomes another desire.

Now here is the clue for you:

If you want to get on a plane or go to a movie, then you have to buy a ticket. This ticket needs to be given at the door. If you hold onto the ticket, how will you go in?

If you want to be admitted to a college, then you need an application form. You fill it out and then you must submit it; you cannot hold onto it.

Likewise on the journey of life, you have to keep submitting your desires and not hold onto them. And as you keep submitting your desires, then fewer desires come up.

Unfortunate are those who keep on desiring and yet their desires are not fulfilled;

A little more fortunate are those whose desires get fulfilled over a long period of time;

More fortunate are those whose desires get fulfilled as soon as they arise;

The most fortunate are those who have no desires because there is fulfillment before a desire can arise.

✍ **News Flash:**

Sri Sri is still in Rishikesh, where 350 people arrived from all over India for the Advanced Course—a hundred more than expected. The volunteers ran around arranging rooms at the ashrams. During Satsang the hall spilled over with participants, their faces radiating ecstasy in the Master's presence.

Today is Gudi Padwa and Ugadi—the new year celebrated in many parts of India. All 350 devotees went for a dip in the holy Ganges at 4:30 AM with Guruji oblivious to the icy temperature of the water.

Swami Pragyanandji, the renowned 75-year old saint of Rishikesh, had a vision in which he saw Sri Sri as Brahma, Vishnu, and Mahesh (Shiva). He then performed a puja to Guruji.

March 26, 1996
Bangalore Ashram, India

42 Blame and Misery

When a worldly man is miserable, he blames the people around him, the system, and the world in general.

When a seeker is miserable, he also blames the world, but in addition he blames the Path, the Knowledge, and himself.

It is better not to be a seeker so that you blame less. But then, a seeker *(sadhak)* also enjoys everything much more. There is more love in life and more pain. When there is more joy, the contrast is greater.

A certain level of maturity is needed to see things as they are and not to blame the Path, the Self, or the world.

Do you see what I am saying?

If one jumps across this threshold of blame and misery, then there is no fall. It is like a quantum leap.

The Divine does not test you. Testing is part of ignorance. Who will test? One who does not know something will test, isn't it? God knows your capacity, so why should He have to test you?

Then, why the misery? It is for *thithiksha*, forbearance in you. And forbearance can be increased by prayerful surrender —or a vigorous challenge to your patience! *(laughter)*

✍ **News Flash:**

The grand finale to the Rishikesh course: a picnic to Neelkant Hills and holy Haridwar, followed by a wild Satsang in New Delhi. Sri Sri is now back at the Ashram for a quiet three days before his Australian tour.

News from the U.K.: Sri Sri had given a rose to a lady on February 13. She called to say that the flower is still amazingly fresh and fragrant after six weeks! This miracle inspired an otherwise unwilling lady to take the Healing Breath Workshop.

Important exercise: Find out what it is that has been with you forever. Belma says that she asked herself this question twenty years ago and she knows all the answers. And that there is only one answer...

April 3, 1996
Sydney, Australia

43 Attachments

ATTACHMENTS CAUSE FEVERISH BREATH AND FEVERISH breath takes away peace of mind. Then you are in pieces and fall prey to misery.

Before you get scattered too much, gather yourself and rid your breath of the feverishness through surrender and sadhana (spiritual practices). Unfortunately, most people do not notice this until it is too late.

When someone is drowning in the ocean of attachments, surrender is the life jacket they can put on and wait for the rescue team. Without fighting the attachments, observe the feverish breath and go to the cool place of silence within.

Your first step in this direction is directing your attachment to the Knowledge, to the Divine.

Your non-attachment to the mundane is your charm.
Your attachment to the Divine is your beauty.

✍ **News Flash:**

Thursday was Rama's birthday, so Sri Sri gave a stunning talk on Rama. At the Madras Satsang, many dignitaries, including the former President of India and his family, came to receive the Master's blessings. Brilliant questions and answers created a moving Satsang.

Singapore snatched a Satsang on the way to Australia.

Perth packed them in and Sydney was swirling. Two religious fundamentalists verbally attacked Sri Sri as soon as he entered the hall, shocking the audience. Unshaken, Guruji delivered a powerful and compassionate discourse.

✍ *Sri Sri was sitting in the airport in Perth, Western Australia, when he asked Joy what she does.*

"I'm an interior decorator,"she said.

"Oh, we do the same job," he replied.

April 10, 1996
Jakarta, Indonesia

44 Vivek

When you follow fun, misery follows you...
When you follow Knowledge, fun follows you.

If you say that you have no one in this world, then you are disowning me. And if you disown me, then I cannot do anything for you.

Vivek means knowing that everything is changing. Time and again you have to awaken to this—that the world, the people, our body, our emotions, are constantly changing.

When you experience sorrow, understand that vivek has been overshadowed.

Question: What am I here for?
Sri Sri: Find out what you are *not* here for:

1. You are not here to blame;
2. You are not here to cry;
3. You are not here to sleep;
4. You are not here to show off;
5. You are not here to fight;
6. You are not here to be miserable;
7. You are not here to be angry;
8. You are not here to worry.

✍ **News Flash:**

In Melbourne, Australia, Sri Sri activated the fire alarm, and at the airport he activated the metal detector. After a beautiful Advanced Course, Guruji is now in joyful Jakarta, where Kim and her entourage greeted the Master with great fanfare at the airport. He later blessed the land for a new Ashram, an initiative taken by our dear Kim's husband, Mr. Tolani. Jakarta is vibrating with four Satsangs a day and flooding with tears of joy and devotion.

April 18, 1996
Bali Cliff Resort, Bali, Indonesia

45 Words

We attach meaning to words and we distort them, too. For example, the word *brainwashing*. Like your body, your brain needs washing sometimes. You don't want to walk around with a dirty brain, a dirty mind. What is wrong with the word *brainwashing?* It indicates a clean brain, a clean mind. But it is used in a derogatory manner.

Like that, the word *disillusionment*. It is good that you are disillusioned. You have come to reality.

Like *purana*. It means *that which is new in the town, the most modern*. But today it is used in the sense of being old.

In the course of time, meanings of words change. The word *enthused* comes from the Greek which means *God is with us*. Then it came to mean *crazy*, and now it's changed again.

Don't be stuck with the words. Your worries are words. Your ideas are words. Wisdom is beyond words. It is the very Being. It is the essence of all words. See and relate beyond words. Then there is no lie in your life.

If you manipulate words, it is a lie;
If you play on words, it is a joke;
If you rely on words, it is ignorance;
If you transcend words, it is wisdom.

✍ **News Splash:**

Sri Sri received a royal welcome at the resort with traditional Balinese dance and garlands. Press and TV crews invaded the hotel and splashed the news throughout Indonesia. Guruji put all the press people into silent meditation and they came out with big smiles. Now they are arranging courses.

A thousand stars reflected over the Indian Ocean and the cliff-side pool. The silence generated from our course was so profound that the hotel staff themselves spontaneously started observing silence, communicating with us only through gestures and notes. Mr. and Mrs. Tolani and their team did an outstanding job.

We enjoyed a sumptuous farewell dinner outside by the lotus pools, followed by a Balinese dance drama from the Ramayana. Drops began to fall from the heavens during our lively Satsang; by evening's end we were singing and dancing in the rain with the Master.

April 24, 1996
Bangalore Ashram, India

46 Karma

STRANGE ARE THE WAYS OF KARMA. THE MORE YOU UNDERSTAND it, the more amazed you become. It brings people together and separates them. It causes some to be weak and some to be strong. It makes some rich and some poor. All the struggle in the world, whatever it may be, is the bondage of karma. It cuts across all logic and reasoning. This understanding will lift you from getting stuck to the events or personalities and help you in your journey to the Self.

Question: So a thief can say it is my karma to steal?
Sri Sri: Then the police have the karma to catch him too! *(laughter)*

Only human life has the ability to be free from karma. And only a few thousands aim to be free from it. Performing actions cannot eliminate karma.

Only through Grace can the bondage of karma be burnt.

News Splash:

In Bali at sunset, we swam under a rainbow in a cliffside pool overlooking the Indonesian Ocean.

We visited many temples on the ocean coast. The local people honored Sri Sri by taking him into an ancient Shiva temple which does not allow tourists.

Huge crowds welcomed Sri Sri in Singapore. Scores of people had to be turned away from a public utility auditorium. Chinese musicians, Indian dancers, and many dignitaries were present, including ministers and officials of Singapore and Malaysia. Guruji gave four wonderful Satsangs a day in devotees' homes, with delightfully delicious food everywhere. Many Art of Living courses are now in progress, including those in the corporate sector. The tour's highlight was a living room Satsang with a rapid-fire and awakening talk on the Upanishads that left everyone spellbound and speechless.

After a lightning Satsang in Madras, Sri Sri is back at the Ashram for a series of celebrations.

May 2, 1996
Bangalore Ashram, India

47 Sanyas & Your Associations

SANYAS MEANS WHAT?

I am nothing and I want nothing, or

I am *everything* and I have *everything*.

Sanyas is being colorless or multicolored.

Your associations or company can either elevate you or push you down. Company causes first an attraction and then delusion. This keeps your mind swinging between the two extremes and causes love and hatred. With the power of Knowledge and Satsang, you can rise above this dilemma.

News Flash:

Late news: Sri Sri took over fifty people to see the night safari in Singapore, the only night safari in the world. The guide kept saying that our group was unusually lucky because every animal in the forest came near the tram "to take darshan!" The local people were so surprised.*

In India, eight prominent saints honored Sri Sri in a private meeting at one of their ashrams. Each saint gives lectures or darshan to hundreds of thousands of devotees and they each run their

**blessings from the glimpse of the Master*

own schools, hospitals and ashrams. Four of them, who were just introduced to the Master, followed us for a brief tour of our Bangalore Ashram, where the skies opened and grace poured down in buckets this week. While Sri Sri and the saints were all on the top of the hill at Sumeru Mantap, lightning and thunder surrounded us. Everyone got drenched and ran to Guruji's kutir. Immediately these very popular and formal Sanyasis began to shed their orange garments. But what to give them to wear? Soon they were all wearing Guruji's white dhotis and being fed by his hand, looking more like a group of joyful children happy to be home again. Somehow in their new clothes they began to relax and smile and laugh, and soon they were radiating the Master's grace from deep inside. All of us were awed to see how the formal heads of institutions were transformed. As they left, they humbly asked for Sri Sri's blessings and invited him to their ashrams. They said, "Mother Nature gave us all a bath before we entered your temple, Guruji."

The first Advanced Course has started at the Ashram.

May 9, 1996
Bangalore Ashram, India

48 Illusion

Illusion is error of perception, and knowing illusion as illusion is Knowledge.

Our experience of the world is based on perception. Since every perception is erroneous, the world is an illusion. Experiences are all of perception. The experiencer is the only reality.

Look for the seer, the experiencer, in between experiences. Every experience leaves a hangover and clouds the intellect.

Wake up this moment. Shake your head of all past experiences and look at the pure Being that I am and that you are.

Question: How do you distinguish the experience and the experiencer?

Sri Sri: Are you really all here? Are you listening? Now close your eyes and see who is listening, who is questioning, who is sitting, and who wants what? Who is confused? You may not get any answer but that is fine. Never mind.

News Flash:

A Chinese movie maker tried his level best to sign up Sri Sri for his latest blockbuster. Guruji said, "I don't know acting," and the movie maker said, "Just be natural, accept the situation as it is, take responsibility, be 100%." The movie is about a wise man who brought Buddhism to China. The movie maker said that through this mega-performance, the Art of Living would reach the whole of China. Guruji winked at his devotees and said, "Should I change my profession?"

The first Advanced Course ended and the second has begun. The Ashram is bustling with people. Every inch of space is occupied—three times the holding capacity of the Ashram and yet no complaints. No chaos! So smooth! Only laughter and new songs have filled Sumeru Mantap.

✍ Sri Sri's 40th birthday is May 13, 1996

Let us keep the Master specially in our awareness this day. If we prepare a meal, let it be a meal worthy to serve him. If we go to a movie, let it be a movie we would take him to see. When we speak of others, let us speak only the kind words we would say in his presence. Let us celebrate together the fullness of his grace on this special day.

May 16, 1996
Bangalore Ashram, India

49 Self

SELF IS NOT JUST THE MIND-BODY COMPLEX. OFTEN PEOPLE think of the Self as the mind-body complex.

This is an erroneous notion. Neither the body nor the mind is the Self. All the yoga you do is for the body. All the meditation you do is for the mind.

Whether calm or disturbed,
your mind remains mind.
Whether sick or well,
your body remains body.
Self is all-encompassing.

Service without attitude
Love without reason
Knowledge without intellect
Life beyond time and events
IS WHAT YOU ARE.

The only purpose for this body to exist is to make you aware of how beautiful you are—and to make you aware that it is possible to live all the values you cherish and create a world of divinity around you.

✍ **News Flash:**

Tents were pitched to house a thousand devotees who came from all over for Sri Sri's 40th birthday celebration. Sacred Vedic chants enlivened the morning air, and in the evening everyone danced with candles in their hands; Sumeru Mantap looked like a festive cake.

The third Advanced Course has begun.

May 21, 1996
Bangalore Ashram, India

50 Enlightenment

ENLIGHTENMENT IS BEYOND SEASONS LIKE THE EVERgreen coconut tree.

Sometimes the question comes up: "What's the use of all these courses? Your behavior has not changed!"

The Knowledge acquired by a human being cannot be measured or judged by external behavior. Someone may behave as though they have absorbed all the Knowledge, but internally they have not. The reverse is also true. Someone who seems to have not changed at all may have absorbed a lot.

Ordinary people would just look at the behavior, but the intelligent looks beyond and is amazed by the play of the consciousness (Brahman).

Behavior affects relationships;
Attitude affects behavior;
Knowledge or ignorance affects attitude;
Grace brings forth Knowledge.

Your inside is like a tree—in some seasons barren and at other times blossomed. Enlightenment is beyond seasons like the evergreen coconut tree which yields throughout the year.

✍ **News Flash:**

The third Advanced Course (in Tamil) melted not only the heart but also a gallstone of a participant! Many more healings were reported; minds opened, blocked arteries opened also. The rains held off for almost an hour as an intense Satsang was underway in Sumeru Mantap.

Sri Sri is presiding over a large "Conference for Awakening the Society," organized by several spiritual heads of state, before he takes off for Paris.

May 29, 1996
den Haag, Netherlands

51 Samadhi

A SINGLE CELL BECOMES THE WHOLE BODY. SOMEWHERE it is nails, somewhere it is nose and tongue, but all is a manifestation of a single cell. In the same way, the entire universe is made up of a single substance.

Remembering and FEELING that everything is made up of one thing heals the body and mind and balances the *doshas*.* This is *savitarka samadhi. Savitarka samadhi* means *equanimity with logical awareness.*

Deep sleep can be *jada samadhi* (equanimity with inertia). And hence, sleep is the main factor in healing. Even medicines will not help without sleep and rest.

Samadhi with ecstasy has no logic. This is *nirvitarka samadhi,* awareness with bliss.

Nirvitarka samadhi is even beyond the experience of bliss—undefinable, beyond words.

**The three major constitutional types—vata, pitta, and kapha—that make up one's individual body/mind complex, as revealed by the ancient natural health science of Ayurveda.*

✍ **News Flash:**

The Advanced Course was held at the Hotel Leonardo da Vinci, just on the outskirts of Paris. The manager of the hotel expressed that his place was never filled with so much love and light. The Satsang, sightseeing, the feast on the boat, and Paris at night made the entire day a rendezvous with the Divine.

The next morning five cars and a minivan set out for Holland without any proper address. Miraculously, everybody reached the lecture hall in time. Some fumed that they had not been given any address or telephone number. They all cooled down in one minute when Sri Sri smiled and said, "Have trust and fun. If you lose your smile for small things, then what is the use of being with me? It is a double waste of time, yours and mine."

The celebration continued past midnight and this Weekly Knowledge was born.

June 5, 1996
German Academy, Bad Antogast, Germany

52 What You Know

WHAT SHALL WE TALK ABOUT TODAY?

What is the point in talking about something of which you know nothing? There is no point in talking about what you know...and no point in talking about what you don't know! *(laughter)*

Stefano: "What about something you think you know but don't know?"

Sri Sri: "We can talk about something you think you know but you don't know, or something you think you don't know but you know." *(laughter)*

There is no end to learning, but there is an end to unlearning. That is when you become totally hollow and empty.

✍ **Riddle:** *What is something so precious that you lose somewhere and find somewhere else? (Answer next week.)*

✍ **News Flash:**

On the way back from Holland to the German Academy, we had a picnic on the bank of the river Rhine near beautiful Boppard. The Academy was full to capacity with Teacher Training Phase 1 and 2 and the Advanced Course all in full swing.

Our spring water has a mind of its own. It flows for some people and stops for others. When Kirpal goes with Guruji's jug, the water joyfully rushes forth!

June 13, 1996
St. Louis, Missouri

Today marks the end of the first year of the Weekly Knowledge. The year started in Big Sur and is ending in St. Louis; it began in KNOWLEDGE *and is concluding in* SEVA *(selfless service for others). The Weekly Knowledge now goes to over 300 Satsang groups, touching 7,000 people every week around the world.*

53 Seva is Savior

THE WAY TO EXPAND FROM INDIVIDUAL TO UNIVERSAL consciousness is to share others' sorrow and joy. As you grow with time, your consciousness should also grow. When you expand in Knowledge with time, then depression is not possible. Your innermost source is joy.

The way to overcome personal misery is to share universal misery! The way to expand personal joy is to share universal joy. Instead of thinking *What about me? What can I gain from this world?*, think *What can I do for the world?* When everyone comes from the point of contributing to society, you have a Divine society. We have to educate and culture our individual consciousness in order to expand with time in the Knowledge... from *What about me?* to *What can I contribute?*

If you are not having good experiences in meditation, then do more seva—you will gain merit and your meditation will be deeper. When you bring some relief or freedom to someone through seva, good vibrations and blessings come to you.

Seva brings merit;
Merit allows you to go deep in meditation;
Meditation brings back your smile.

✍ **Answer to last week's riddle:**

That something which is so precious to you is your smile—your joy. You lose it in the world and find it in the Self, in Satsang. If you can't find it here, forget about it! You can't find it anywhere.

✍ **News Flash:**

After a quick two-day stopover in Boston with overflowing crowds at Interface and Harvard's Kennedy School of Government and with lively late night Satsangs, Sri Sri arrived in Pittsburgh to a packed schedule of household Satsangs, temple visits, two lectures, and a celebration to inaugurate our new Center, complete with cake flying in all directions!

Linda had this extra joy of having Guruji throw slices of cake all over her immaculate living room. She managed to maintain only a slightly strained smile, knowing that her Master spattered her furniture with love to point out her overattachment to order. Had anyone else done this, they would have been in big trouble.

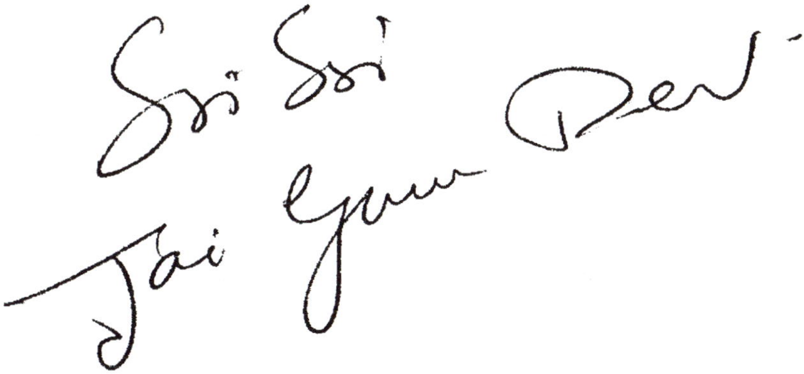

The **Art of Living Foundation** is devoted to making your life a celebration. We are a non-profit educational organization run entirely by volunteers and are accredited as an official NGO with the United Nations. We offer workshops for spiritual growth and self-development that allow busy people to take advantage of Sri Sri's multi-dimensional teachings. We sponsor service projects worldwide, including rehabilitative training for prisoners, programs for individuals living with HIV and cancer, and vocational training for rural women in Asia. Our "Dollar-a-Day" program provides over 500 children with food, clothing and schooling.

▲ You can visit our web site on the Internet at: **http://www.artofliving.org**

▲ **The Healing Breath Workshop** is the ideal introduction to Sri Sri's teachings. This 16-18 hour program over 4-6 days has changed the lives of thousands.

Breath contains the secret of life. Breath is linked to the vital energy in us, or *prana.* Low prana translates into depression, lethargy, dullness, and poor enthusiasm. When our mind and body are charged with prana, we feel alert, energetic, and full of good humor. Specific breathing techniques revitalize our prana and enhance our physical and emotional health.

The Healing Breath Workshop is a weekend of direct experience and practical knowledge in the Art of Living. At its heart is *Sudarshan Kriya,* a unique breathing practice and a potent energizer that fully oxygenates the cells and recharges them with new life. Negative emotions—stored as toxins in the body—are easily uprooted and flushed out. Tensions, frustrations, and anger get released. Anxiety, depression, and lethargy are washed away. The mind is left calm and centered with a clearer vision of the world, our relationships, and ourselves.

Sudarshan Kriya is simple to learn and practice. To take the Healing Breath Workshop, contact the Art of Living Center nearest you *(see directory, page 96).*

▲ **Sahaj Samadhi Meditation**

Not one of us lacks spiritual depth. The peace and happiness we feverishly seek in the world are already contained within us, covered only by the clouds of stress and strain. These clouds are lifted with Sahaj Samadhi meditation—a gift of wisdom from Sri Sri. Sahaj Samadhi meditation provides a rest much deeper than sleep. Like awakening renewed on a sunny morning, your outlook on life changes completely towards the positive. Stress drops off, the chattering mind becomes serene and creative, aging slows, and you rediscover the unshakable contentment of your inner Self. Sahaj Samadhi meditation is easy to learn and practice. With simple guidance, anyone can meditate. Personal instruction is offered at Art of Living Centers worldwide.

▲ **Art of Living Advanced Courses** are specially designed for those who have completed the Healing Breath Workshop. These in-residence retreat programs provide a welcome opportunity to dive deep into inner silence with advanced meditation practices. Various games and processes keep everybody guessing what will come next. Each evening ends with a celebration of singing, dancing, and marvelous wisdom. Participants leave feeling renewed emotionally and elevated spiritually, with a dynamic freshness for greater success.

Some Advanced Courses are offered in Sri Sri's presence; meeting the Master is the experience of a lifetime...

▲ **Books, videos, and audiotapes of Sri Sri** are now available by mail. Titles include: *The Way of Grace, God Loves Fun, The Meaning of Life, The Nature of Enlightenment, Om Shanti, The Path of Love, Peace is Our Nature, What is a Guru?,* and the *Yoga Sutras of Patanjali.* For a catalog, call or write:

Art of Living Books and Tapes
P.O. Box 80068, Portland, OR 97280-1068
Toll Free: (800) 574-3001
Outside USA: (503) 227-6411

ART OF LIVING FOUNDATION CENTERS: USA National Headquarters (805) 563-6396 / Arizona Tucson (520) 579-0414; **California** Apple Valley (619) 240-1222; Big Sur (408) 667-2398; Los Angeles (310) 820-9429; Oakland (514) 530-5464; Orange County (714) 493-4574; Salinas (408) 758-9646; San Diego (619) 581-9011; San Jose (415) 964-8908; Santa Barbara (805) 563-6396; **Colorado** Boulder (303) 652-8294; Cascade (719) 684-8003; Colorado Springs (719) 488-9478; Denver (303) 333-3031; **Connecticut** Woodbridge (203) 397-0510; **District of Columbia** (301) 585-9126; **Florida** Ft. Myers (941) 334-4294; Miami/Ft. Lauderdale (954) 721-7437; Orlando (407) 324-5852; **Georgia** Atlanta (770) 937-9323; **Hawaii** Kaua'i (808) 826-5595; Oahu (808) 944-3323; **Illinois** Chicago (847) 564-5947; **Indiana** (800) 897-5913; **Iowa** Fairfield (515) 472-2053; Iowa City (319) 358-9201; **Kansas** (800) 897-5913; **Maryland** Baltimore (410) 527-0768; Silver Spring (301) 585-9126; **Massachusetts** Boston (617) 354-5566; Cape Cod (508) 349-3591; **Michigan** Flint (810) 736-4838; **Minnesota** Minneapolis (612) 786-1688; **Missouri** Kirksville (816) 665-3004; St. Louis (314) 576-5665; **Montana** Bozeman (406) 586-7181; **Nebraska** (800) 897-5913; **Nevada** Lake Tahoe (702)-721-5879; Las Vegas (702) 897-9177; **New Jersey** Somerset (908) 560-3521; **New Mexico** Albuquerque (505) 255-7496; Grants (505) 876-2564; Santa Fe (505) 984-0327; **New York** Lagrangeville (914) 677-5871; Manhattan (212) 353-9252; Queens (718) 428-5599; **North Dakota** (800) 897-5913; **Ohio** Cleveland (440) 243-7427; **Oregon** Portland (503) 452-4237; **Pennsylvania** Philadelphia (215) 247-3305; Pittsburgh (412) 729-3476; **South Dakota** (800) 897-5913; **Texas** Dallas (972) 517-2213; Houston (713) 564-2216; San Antonio (210) 537-4875; **Virginia** Arlington (703) 671-8642; **Washington** Seattle (425) 746-2779; **West Virginia** (800) 897-5913; **Wisconsin** (800) 897-5913; **Wyoming** Wilson (307) 734-1034; **INTERNATIONAL CENTERS: Australia** Weston (61) 06 287-4004; **Belorussia** Minsk 375-17-2729117; **Canada** Ashram (819) 532-3328; Montreal (514) 670-5728; Halifax (902) 422-3411; Ottawa (613) 749-1880; Vancouver (604) 228-8728; **China** (886) 2-881-2882; **Costa Rica** fax (506) 487-7020; **Crotia** 385-52-773505; **Denmark** 45-33-323545; **England** 44-181-9587189; **France** 33-5490-28543; **Germany** 49-7804-910923; **Hong Kong** (852) 2762-1811; **India** (91) 80-6645-106; **Italy** 39-55-4491631; **Lithuania** 370-33-55541; **Malaysia** 03-442070; **Mauritius** (230) 6764557; **Netherlands** 31-72-5152240; **Norway** 47-22-364083, artofliving@oslo.mail.telia.com; **Panama** 265-1333 & 236-3565; **Poland** 48-22-6437544; **St. Lucia** 758-452-5320; **Singapore** 65-337-2341, 65-348-6280; **Slovenia** 386-61-343992; **Sweden** 48-8-7022431; **Switzerland** 41-71-9117583; **Trinidad** 809-665-9611